P9-CAN-182

ELIZABETH I

— QUEEN OF ENGLAND —

ELIZABETH I
QUEEN OF ENGLAND

BARBARA GOTTFRIED HOLLANDER

Britannica
Educational Publishing

IN ASSOCIATION WITH

ROSEN
EDUCATIONAL SERVICES

This book is dedicated to the three strongest women I know, my grandmother (Jean Zelcer), my mother (Danuta Zelcer Gottfried), and my daughter (Ruthie Danielle).

Published in 2018 by Britannica Educational Publishing (a trademark of Encyclopædia Britannica, Inc.) in association with The Rosen Publishing Group, Inc.
29 East 21st Street, New York, NY 10010

Distributed exclusively by Rosen Publishing.
To see additional Britannica Educational Publishing titles, go to rosenpublishing.com.

First Edition

Britannica Educational Publishing
J.E. Luebering: Executive Director, Core Editorial
Andrea R. Field: Managing Editor, Compton's by Britannica

Rosen Publishing
Heather Moore Niver: Editor
Nelson Sá: Art Director
Michael Moy: Designer
Cindy Reiman: Photography Manager
Heather Moore Niver: Photo Researcher

Library of Congress Cataloging-in-Publication Data

Names: Hollander, Barbara Gottfried, 1970- author.
Title: Elizabeth I : queen of England / Barbara Gottfried Hollander.
Description: First edition. | New York, NY : Britannica Educational Publishing, 2017. | Series: Women who changed history | Includes bibliographical references and index.
Identifiers: LCCN 2016057942| ISBN 9781680486438 (library bound : alk. paper) | ISBN 9781680486414 (pbk. : alk. paper) | ISBN 9781680486421 (6-pack : alk. paper)
Subjects: LCSH: Elizabeth I, Queen of England, 1533-1603—Juvenile literature. | Great Britain—History—Elizabeth, 1558-1603—Juvenile literature. | Queens—Great Britain—Biography—
Juvenile literature.
Classification: LCC DA355 .H57 2017 | DDC 942.05/5092 [B] —dc23
LC record available at https://lccn.loc.gov/2016057942

Manufactured in the United States of America

Photo credits: Cover, p. 34 Print Collector/Hulton Fine Art Collection/Getty Images; p. 7 SuperStock/Getty Images; pp. 9, 27, 38 Photos.com/Thinkstock; p. 10 Popperfoto/Getty Images; p. 11 The Protected Art Archive/Alamy Stock Photo; p. 13 Collection Christophel/Alamy Stock Photo; pp. 15, 22 Universal Images Group/Getty Images; p. 19 Print Collector/Hulton Archive /Getty Images; pp. 20–21 Houses of Parliament,Westminster, London, UK/Bridgeman Images; p. 24 Library of Congress Prints and Photograph Division; p. 25 AF archive/Alamy Stock Photo; p. 29 Private Collection/Bridgeman Images; pp. 30–31 Universal History Archive/Universal Images Group/Getty Images; p. 32 Hulton Archive/Getty Images; p. 36 TonyBaggett/iStock /Thinkstock; p. 39 Digital Image Library/Alamy Stock Photo; p. 40 Collection of the New-York Historical Society, USA/Bridgeman Images; p. 42 Hardwick Hall, Derbyshire, UK/National Trust Photographic Library/PA Burton/Bridgeman Images.

CONTENTS

INTRODUCTION

King Henry VIII of England thought men made the best rulers. He wanted a son to take his place as king. The English ruler tried almost everything to have a male heir. Henry VIII's quest began at the age of seventeen when he married twenty-three-year-old Catherine of Aragon. Catherine was the widow of Henry's brother, Arthur. In those days, people married very young. At the time of Catherine's first wedding, she was only fifteen years old, and Henry's brother was fourteen.

While Catherine's first marriage lasted only one year, she and Henry VIII were married for twenty-four years. During this time, Catherine was pregnant six times in nine years. She only had one surviving child—a girl named Mary. Desperate for a son, Henry ended his marriage to Catherine and married a woman named Anne Boleyn. When Anne was pregnant, letters were sent out announcing the arrival of a boy. But Anne had a girl instead. The baby was named Elizabeth, after both of her parents' grandmothers.

When Elizabeth was only two years old, Henry had Anne killed by beheading. Days after the execution, Henry married again. He chose Jane Seymour as his wife. Because Jane had six brothers, Henry thought she would be more likely to have a son. After eighteen months of marriage, Jane gave birth to a son named Edward, but she died shortly after childbirth. Henry then married three more times, but he did not have any more sons. Upon Henry VIII's death, Edward became king at the age of nine, but he died six years later.

Painted by Marcus Gheeraerts the Younger, this portrait of Elizabeth was commissioned by Sir Henry Lee. Elizabeth stands on the world, with her feet on Oxfordshire, where Lee resided.

At the time Henry and Catherine were married, England was a Roman Catholic country. The Roman Catholic Church did not recognize divorces. To end his marriage, Henry went against the church, breaking away from it to establish an independent Church of England. Henry's actions resulted in great religious battles within the country. Catherine refused to accept both the annulment that canceled their marriage and Henry's later marriage to Anne. Catherine reportedly proclaimed, "I am Queen, and Queen I will die." Henry VIII responded by no longer allowing Catherine to see their daughter Mary.

Henry VIII caused great suffering to his six wives and their children in his quest for a male heir. His actions also brought about tremendous religious and political upheaval in England. Like many of his time, Henry believed that men were better rulers. Yet it was Henry and Catherine's daughter, Elizabeth, who is remembered as one of England's greatest monarchs. She rose to power at a time when men dominated the political scene, and her reign was one of England's most prosperous periods. Despite her father's obsession with a male heir, it was a woman who became one of England's greatest rulers.

CHAPTER ONE

A QUEEN IS BORN

On September 7, 1533, Anne Boleyn gave birth to Elizabeth in Greenwich, England. The new princess had fair skin, wavy red hair, and dark brown eyes. Her full name was Elizabeth Tudor. Her grandfather, Henry VII, was the first Tudor king, having defeated King Richard III in war. At birth, Elizabeth was next in line to become the ruler of England. But all that changed when Elizabeth's mother was killed in 1536 and her father, Henry VIII, declared Elizabeth illegitimate (her parents' marriage was no longer recognized as legal).

Several paintings of Anne Boleyn hang in London's National Portrait Gallery. Many were painted in the 1500s by unknown artists.

EARLY YEARS

At three months old, Elizabeth was sent away from her parents to live in the Royal Palace of Hatfield. Located about 20 miles (32 kilometers) from London, this palace was also home to Elizabeth's older half-sister, Mary, and later to her younger half-brother, Edward. The children were under the care of nurses and tutors. Henry VIII neglected his children. Lady Margaret Bryan once had to write to the king to ask for new clothes, because Elizabeth's were much too small for her.

Around 1540, Hans Holbein painted this portrait of King Henry VIII, who was the second Tudor monarch and became king at the age of eighteen.

When Elizabeth was only two, her father ordered that her mother be killed by beheading. Henry accused Anne Boleyn of adultery. Most historians believe the charges were made up to give Henry an opportunity to remarry. The last time Elizabeth saw her mother was probably the Christmas before her mother died.

Elizabeth was raised in the Royal Palace of Hatfield, away from her parents, but with her half-sister Mary and half-brother Edward.

With the death of her mother, Elizabeth's life changed overnight in many ways. Without her mother, Elizabeth was declared illegitimate, like her sister Mary. Henry had his marriages to both of their mothers, Catherine and Anne, declared null and void. This meant that both girls were no longer considered heirs to the royal throne. Mary also blamed Anne Boleyn for her troubles and transferred this blame onto Elizabeth. This resentment would later cause Mary to treat Elizabeth badly.

Until the age of four, Lady Bryan continued to take care of Elizabeth. Then Katherine Champernowne, or Kat, took over Elizabeth's care. As a child, Elizabeth learned several subjects, such as history, geography, architecture, and horseback riding. She was a bright student. One of her tutors,

THE FAMOUS ANNE BOLEYN

Henry VIII fell in love with Anne Boleyn. In 1533, Anne and Henry married in a secret ceremony. But their marriage quickly fell apart because Henry had mistresses and Anne did not have any sons who survived. Henry wanted to end his marriage to Anne so he could marry one of his mistresses, Jane Seymour. The king made accusations against Anne, including adultery and treason. Henry then had Anne thrown into the Tower of London.

Thomas Cromwell helped the king accuse Anne, her family, and her friends. Anne's long-time friend, Mark Smeaton, was probably tortured into helping the king. Anne's friend, Sir Henry Norris, and her brother, George, were also arrested. Both George and Anne were put on trial. Although there was little evidence of their guilt, both were found guilty and sentenced to death. Anne was beheaded on May 19, 1536. Two days earlier, both her brother and her friend, Mark, were also beheaded at Tower Hill.

Some books, television series, and movies feature Anne Boleyn, including *Anne of the Thousand Days*, *The Tudors*, and *The Other Boleyn Girl*. She remains one of history's most talked about characters. But are the depictions close to the real Anne? Was she really charming, passionate, and hot-tempered? Did she really plot to become queen? Was she guilty of the charges against her? Anne was not well liked as queen of England and she may have used her charms to woo the king, but most agree Anne was not guilty of the charges that led to her beheading.

The film version of *The Other Boleyn Girl* (2008) depicts Anne's journey to queenhood, featuring Natalie Portman as Anne Boleyn and Eric Bana as Henry VIII.

Roger Ashram, once said, "I have dealt with many learned ladies, but amongst them all the brightest star is my illustrious Elizabeth." He would later remark that "her mind has no womanly weakness." His words showed the sexist thinking, or discrimination against women, that dominated Elizabeth's time.

Elizabeth's strengths included music and language. By the age of eleven, Elizabeth knew seven languages well: Latin, Greek, Spanish, French, Italian, Flemish, and English. Elizabeth received an education that was not available to most women in the sixteenth century. She gained valuable knowledge from sharing some of her half-brother's tutors from Cambridge University. Elizabeth's royal education would later help her as queen when dealing with other countries.

THE RELIGIOUS DIVIDE

Elizabeth grew up during a time of religious conflict in England. Before Henry VIII's annulment to Catherine, England was a Roman Catholic nation. The Catholic religion did not believe in divorce. But Henry wanted to end his marriage to Catherine. So he asked Pope Clement VII, who as head of the Roman Catholic Church had authority over the Church of England, to make an exception and annul his union. After the pope refused, Henry eventually reacted with the Act of Supremacy in 1534. This new act declared Henry himself to be the Supreme Head of the Church of England, and anyone who denied this title was guilty of treason. The monasteries throughout England were dissolved and their

Born Giulio di Giuliano de Medici, Clement VII was pope from 1523 to 1534. Henry VIII wanted Pope Clement VII to annul his marriage to Catherine of Aragon.

vast lands and goods turned over to the king, who in turn granted those estates to noblemen who would support his policies. The result was a great expansion of Henry's power. In the northern part of the kingdom, the people rose in rebellion on behalf of the monks, but the Pilgrimage of Grace, as it was called, was put down.

Even though Henry cut ties with the pope and the city of Rome, he wanted the people of England to remain basically Catholic in their piety and belief. He passed the Act of Six Articles (1539), which kept many of the old religious beliefs. These beliefs, called the Catholic Doctrine, included communion, private masses, unmarried priests, and confession. If someone did not believe in the Catholic Doctrine, he or she could be labeled a heretic. The punishment for a heretic was being burned alive while tied to a stake, or wooden pole.

Many of the people accused of being heretics were members of another branch of Christianity called Protestantism. This branch began in 1517 when German theologian Martin Luther hung a document called the Ninety-five Theses, or propositions, on the Wittenberg Castle church door. Luther's document listed the abuses of the Roman Catholic Church, like the sale of indulgences. This practice claimed that a person could rid him or herself of sin by giving money to the church. Martin Luther also introduced two main ideas. He claimed the Bible was the religious authority and that salvation is possible though faith alone.

Luther's ideas challenged the Catholic Church, which reacted aggressively against those supporting them. People were tried and killed for believing and practicing Protestant beliefs. As Protestantism took hold in Europe, Catholic and

Protestant countries went to war. Inside England, the Catholics and Protestants fought for control of the country. Within the Tudor family, the rulers did not even agree. After the separation from Rome, Henry persecuted with equal severity the Catholics who adhered to the Roman church and the Protestants who rejected its doctrines. When his daughter Mary came to the throne, she ardently supported Roman Catholicism, but Edward and Elizabeth favored Protestantism.

CHAPTER TWO

AGAINST ALL ODDS

Henry VIII married a total of six times. He used annulments to end some of his marriages, which caused his children to lose their place in the royal line of succession. These actions caused a lot of bad feelings between his children. A difference in religion also caused conflict. While both Edward and Elizabeth supported the rise of Protestantism in England, Mary was fiercely loyal to the Roman Catholic Church. Many Catholics, like Mary, did not want Elizabeth as queen of England.

TROUBLE WITH BLOODY MARY

To marry Anne Boleyn, Henry annulled his marriage to Catherine of Aragon. After this annulment, neither Catherine nor their daughter, Mary, was part of the royal family. They were not even allowed to see each other anymore. Both Catherine and Mary viewed Anne as the cause of their troubles. When Anne died, Mary transferred her bad feelings to Anne's daughter, Elizabeth. Seventeen years apart, Mary and Elizabeth were both declared illegitimate. This meant neither daughter was allowed to become the next ruler of England.

But all of this changed with Henry's marriage to his sixth wife, Catherine Parr. She encouraged Henry to become closer to all of his children and make them eligible to rule England again. Mary could now become queen, after her half-brother, Edward, died at the age of fifteen. When Mary ruled, she was not kind to Elizabeth for several reasons. Firstly, Elizabeth's mother had taken the place of Mary's mother. Secondly, Mary, like her mother Catherine, was very loyal to the Catholic Church, but Elizabeth supported the Protestants. Thirdly, Elizabeth was competition, because she was also in line for the throne.

Knowing that she was in danger, Elizabeth went back to Hatfield. After Mary

CATHERINE OF ARAGON

Catherine of Aragon was the daughter of Ferdinand and Isabella of Spain. She was married to Henry VIII and, earlier, to his older brother.

Created by John Byam Liston Shaw, this painting depicts Princess Elizabeth (*right*) and her half-sister, Queen Mary, arriving in London in 1553.

agreed to marry another devout Catholic, Philip II of Spain, who was heir to the Spanish throne, a Protestant rebellion occurred. Sir Thomas Wyatt the Younger joined a group that fought to oppose the marriage. He was eventually captured, taken to the Tower of London, and sentenced to death. Before dying, he announced that Elizabeth did not have anything to do with the rebellion. Still, Elizabeth remained in danger.

Mary imprisoned Elizabeth in the Tower of London during the Wyatt rebellion. Then Mary released Elizabeth and made her a prisoner in Woodstock Manor for one year. Eventually, Elizabeth was put under house arrest in Hatfield. Throughout Mary's reign, the punishments for heresy were brought back. Hundreds of Protestants were burned alive. This earned Mary the nickname "Bloody Mary." In 1558, Mary died of cancer. Because Mary did not have children, her half-sister, Elizabeth, was next in line to assume the throne.

Elizabeth is pictured in her coronation robes. She became queen of England in 1558 and ruled until 1603. Elizabeth was the last of the Tudor monarchs.

BECOMING QUEEN

On November 17, 1558, Elizabeth became queen at the age of twenty-five. She inherited a country at war both with another country and within itself. England was at war with France, which cost England a lot of money. During Mary's rule, her husband King Philip began this war. A French attack on a place called Calais, on the coast of northern France, caused England to lose this land, which had been in its possession since 1347. England was also still suffering from internal fighting between the Catholics and the Protestants.

Upon becoming queen, Elizabeth took care of both conflicts. First, an advisor named William Cecil helped Queen Elizabeth to end the war with France without upsetting Spain. Secondly, she helped pass an act that brought back the Church of England and created a common prayer book. Queen Elizabeth was a Protestant who supported this branch of Christianity within England. But unlike Mary, Elizabeth did not severely impose her religious ideas on the country. Still some Catholics suffered because of their practices. In 1570, Pope Pius V excommunicated Elizabeth, or cut her off from the Catholic Church.

Like many kings and queens, Elizabeth faced trouble from people who posed possible threats to her rule. Elizabeth had a cousin named Mary Stuart (known as Mary, Queen of Scots). In 1568, after being accused of having had a part in the murder of her husband, Lord Darnley, Mary Stuart was forced to abdicate the Scottish throne in favor of her infant son, James VI. Her supporters were later defeated at

Mary, Queen of Scots, portrayed here by artist J. B. Wandesford, was viewed by many Catholics as the rightful heir to the English throne.

the Battle of Langside, and Mary fled from Scotland to England to seek Elizabeth's help. But Elizabeth faced a dilemma. Should she help her cousin and give her refuge? Or should she follow the advice of Parliament and many of her own councilors and have Mary—the woman whom the Roman Catholic Church regarded as the rightful queen of England—executed? Elizabeth chose to have Mary taken into custody while a commission examined her guilt in regard to Darnley's murder.

Many Catholics did not recognize the marriage of Elizabeth's parents, and therefore they did not recognize her right to be queen. There were different attempts by some Catholic supporters to kill Elizabeth. One of these attempts involved letters between Mary Stuart and a plotter named Anthony Babington. After being imprisoned for eighteen years, Mary Stuart was found guilty of treason based on the letters with Babington. She was sentenced to

VIRGIN QUEEN

Elizabeth's father, Henry VIII, had six wives. People marry for different reasons. Henry's multiple marriages were mainly motivated by his desire for a son. But many royal people married to create alliances between countries. An alliance is a group of people (or countries) that work together toward a common goal. For example, when Queen Mary I of England married Philip II of Spain, both countries became unified

The movie *Elizabeth: The Golden Age* starred Cate Blanchett as Elizabeth and Abbie Cornish as Bess Throckmorton, an attendant who secretly married Sir Walter Raleigh, a favorite of the queen.

(continued on the next page)

(continued from the previous page)

under one set of leaders. Mary and Philip worked together to assert Catholicism as the predominant religion in these two countries.

When Elizabeth became queen of England, many men wanted to marry her, including Philip II. Philip hoped to remain in charge of England and keep Catholicism as the main religion. Some of Elizabeth's advisors also thought a marriage between Philip and Elizabeth would help in case France and Scotland formed an alliance. But Elizabeth was not interested in marrying Philip.

Other men also tried to marry Elizabeth, like Prince Erik of Sweden, the Archduke Charles of Austria, the Earl of Arran, and Sir William Pickering, among other suitors. Elizabeth and her advisors thought about these suitors in political and religious terms. For example, Prince Erik was Protestant, but Sweden was not a powerful country that would prove beneficial to England. The Archduke Charles was powerful but Catholic, and Elizabeth wanted England to be more Protestant.

Elizabeth faced a lot of pressure to get married so she could have an heir to the throne. She was the last of the Tudor dynasty. But Elizabeth never married. She remained single throughout her 44-year reign. Elizabeth once declared that she was married to England.

death with a warrant signed by Elizabeth. Sixteen years later, after Elizabeth's death, Mary Stuart's son, King James VI of Scotland, would become King James I of England.

CHAPTER THREE

THE ELIZABETHAN ERA

The forty-four-year reign of Queen Elizabeth I—from 1558 to 1603—is called the Elizabethan era. This time period is also known as the Golden Age of England for several reasons. First, the country experienced peace and stability. Secondly, England grew wealthier because of the period of exploration, as people journeyed to the New World and other lands. Finally, it was a time when painters, poets, and playwrights created volumes of work.

This prayer book's frontispiece shows Queen Elizabeth praying at Bristol. She exercised more tolerance than previous English monarchs.

ENGLAND AND IRELAND

The one big exception to peace in the Elizabethan era was England's conflict with Ireland. As the queen of England, Elizabeth also had authority over Ireland. Ireland was a Roman Catholic country and Elizabeth did not want Ireland to form an alliance with Philip II and Spain. Elizabeth tried to prevent this by tightening control over Ireland. Three failed rebellions during Elizabeth's reign solidified Irish resentment of English rule. The last of these was led by Hugh O'Neill, 2nd earl of Tyrone. As chieftain of the powerful O'Neill family of Ulster, he led skirmishes against the English from 1593 and won the Battle of the Yellow Ford, which sparked a countrywide revolt in 1598. He received aid and troops from Spain but was defeated by the English at Kinsale and forced to surrender in 1603.

Ireland also had a woman who rose to power at a time when men dominated the political scene. Her name was Grace O'Malley. Just as Elizabeth I received an education not usually given to women, O'Malley learned how to sail, a skill generally reserved for men. After her husband's death, O'Malley took control of her family's lands and ships. She led her family's fleets in fights with pirates from Spain, Turkey, and England. She also led a rebellion against Richard Bingham, the English governor of Connaught (a province in western and northwestern Ireland). Grace wanted the right to return to the land of her relatives. After meeting Grace, Elizabeth was impressed and granted her this right.

This illustration portrays a meeting between Grace O'Malley and Elizabeth that took place at Greenwich Castle in September 1593. The women discussed the English-Irish power struggle.

TOWARD PEACE

Elizabeth inherited a country torn by religious differences. She favored and established the Protestant doctrines, but also tried to make concessions to the Catholics to keep the peace. For example, rather than call herself "Supreme Head of the Church of England," Elizabeth chose the title, "Supreme Governor of the Church of England." She also chose to be more moderate in her religious practices and did not support extremists, even within the Protestants. While Puritans (more extreme Protestants) sought to end things like music, dancing, and attending the theater because they viewed them as unholy, Elizabeth fully supported the arts.

During her reign, a real threat came from Spain, which was then viewed as the most powerful country in the world. Under Philip II's rule,

This painting depicts Queen Elizabeth's ride to Tilbury during Philip's attempt to invade England. The defeat of this invasion is one of England's greatest military accomplishments.

Spain had grown very wealthy, in part because of its exploration and exploitation of foreign lands. Elizabeth had refused Philip II's marriage proposal. A Roman Catholic, Philip did not view Henry VIII and Anne's marriage as legally binding. He therefore did not recognize Elizabeth as the rightful heir to the throne and wanted to remove her as queen. After Elizabeth imprisoned Mary, Queen of Scots, Philip prepared a fleet (a group of ships) to invade England and free Mary.

Queen Elizabeth knighted Sir Francis Drake on April 4, 1581, after he successfully traveled around the globe. The ceremony took place on Drake's ship, the *Golden Hind*.

But before Philip attacked, Mary was executed for plotting to kill Elizabeth. Still, Philip planned to invade England. In May 1588, he sent some 130 Spanish ships carrying 2,500 guns and about 20,000 soldiers along the English Channel. This great fleet of ships was known as the Spanish Armada. He planned to join another fleet from the Netherlands in his attack on England. Queen Elizabeth knew about the planned attack. Englishmen waited on the English and Welsh cliffs looking for the Armada so they could declare that the battle would officially begin.

Rather than hide in the palace, Queen Elizabeth rode her white horse to Tilbury, watched her soldiers, and declared that she would "live or die" with them. After eight hours of fighting, the English fleet, commanded by Charles Howard and Sir Francis Drake, won the battle. The queen was celebrated for this victory, which turned England into a superpower and set the stage for a relatively peaceful period.

THE ARTS

Most paintings in the Elizabethan era were portraits, or representations of a person. Many of these portraits were miniature, or smaller in size, and often depicted something personal, like a mistress. Queen Elizabeth's favorite painter was Nicholas Hilliard. Hilliard's first miniature painting of Elizabeth appeared on a playing card in 1572. He also painted *Elizabeth I: The Pelican Portrait*, which features the queen wearing a pelican necklace. This necklace symbolizes Elizabeth's devotion to England. Hilliard later produced

Nicholas Hilliard painted *The Pelican Portrait* when Elizabeth was in her forties. The pelican was thought to represent Elizabeth's selfless love for England.

other paintings of Elizabeth, including *Elizabeth I: The Phoenix Portrait* and *Elizabeth I Playing the Lute*.

The Elizabethan era was also a time when many artists wrote poetry, songs, and plays. Prior to this era, Sir Thomas Wyatt (whose son, Sir Thomas Wyatt the Younger, led an unsuccessful rebellion against Queen Mary I) introduced the Italian sonnet form into English literature. A sonnet is a poem of fourteen lines, with usually ten syllables in each line. Later, this form was changed into the English sonnet (or Shakespearean sonnet), which also contained fourteen lines, but had a specific structure and rhyme scheme. The greatest poet and playwright of the Elizabethan era, William Shakespeare, produced 154 sonnets, many of them about a beautiful woman with dark eyes.

Edmund Spenser was a famous poet of the era who wrote *The Shepheardes Calender* (a poem for each month) and *The Faerie Queene*, which contained political, moral, and fairy tale sections. The translation of several books of Virgil's *Aeneid* by Henry Howard, Earl of Surrey, which appeared in 1557, marked the first use in English of blank verse, a style of unrhymed poetry. The great Elizabethan poet Christopher Marlowe, Shakespeare's most significant predecessor, established blank verse as the medium for later dramatic writing.

Elizabeth agreed to have professional theaters built in England for the first time. During her reign, London had 150,000 to 250,000 people and about 15,000 of them attended the theater weekly. Elizabeth financially backed playwrights, like William Shakespeare. Shakespeare was among the first to portray women as emotionally and intel-

William Shakespeare was an actor and playwright for a company called the Lord Chamberlain's Men. This company was formed during Elizabeth's reign and continued under her successor, King James I.

lectually strong and equal to men. He included references of
Queen Elizabeth in his work, such as in his play *A Midsum-
mer Night's Dream*. Later, after Elizabeth's death, Shakespeare wrote a farewell to his friend and supporter in his
play *Henry VIII*:

> *She [Queen Elizabeth] shall be, to the happiness*
> *of England,*
> *An aged princess; many days shall see her,*
> *And yet no day without a deed to crown it…*
> *A most unspotted lily shall she pass*
> *To the ground, and all the world shall mourn her.*

CHAPTER FOUR

THE GREATEST ENGLISH MONARCH

The phoenix symbolizes virginity and chastity, so this interpretation of Hilliard's painting *The Phoenix Portrait* reinforces that Elizabeth is the Virgin Queen.

Henry VIII wanted a male heir to rule England, but his son, Edward, ruled only for a short time. It was Elizabeth I who finally established England as a superpower. In a time when men were viewed as rational, and women too emotional, Elizabeth came to power and proved that a woman could be the best ruler of England.

HER NATURE

Elizabeth had an independent nature. She made her own decisions. Often,

Queen Elizabeth chose to behave differently than women of that time were expected to, such as playing a more active role in the Spanish battle or not getting married. When her advisors voiced opposing viewpoints, Elizabeth stood by her decisions. Elizabeth's advisors encouraged her to marry and have a Tudor heir to the throne. But after the execution of her third step-mother, Elizabeth declared to her friend Robert Dudley, "I will never marry." (Although she and Dudley later shared a long intimate relationship, Queen Elizabeth I never married him either.)

Elizabeth always had a serious nature. It was said that, at the age of six, Elizabeth had the seriousness of a forty-year-old. This would turn out to be a trait that helped her consider things more logically when deciding matters of religion and war.

The queen was also intelligent and, as a child, had learned much from her half-brother Edward's

Robert Dudley, Earl of Leicester, first met Elizabeth at the age of eight. They shared a lifelong friendship and intimate companionship.

HER
HARD PAST

Elizabeth went through tremendous hardships, such as growing up without a mother and having an absent father; being both imprisoned and placed under house arrest by her half-sister Mary; and living in fear that she would be wrongly implicated in the Protestant rebellion

Emanuel Gottlieb Leutze's painting *Princess Elizabeth in the Tower* depicts Elizabeth's imprisonment in the Tower of London by her half-sister, Queen Mary.

that took place during Mary's reign. Elizabeth had to be strong and courageous to make it through these times. She would later employ these traits to assume the position of queen, ward off dethroning attempts, and fight Philip II and his Spanish Armada.

This difficult upbringing also made her sensitive to the conflicts arising from religious differences. She knew that both her mother and one of her stepmothers, Catherine Parr, favored Protestantism. She also knew that her half-sister, Mary Tudor, was a devout Catholic who, as queen, supported the persecution and killing of Protestants. Elizabeth watched the imprisonments and executions that resulted from religious rebellions, and she lived in fear of being accused of heresy. This encouraged her to take a more moderate position on religion when queen and to be more private with her thoughts.

tutors. Her education would later allow her to understand the politics of both England and other countries.

Finally, Elizabeth was creative, both watching and taking part in the arts. This creativity and love of the arts paved the way for painters, playwrights, and poets.

FAREWELL SPEECH

On November 30, 1601, Queen Elizabeth delivered her last speech, known as her Golden Speech, to the speaker and 140 members of the Commons. Elizabeth was sixty-eight years old and had ruled England for most of her life. The queen's health was poor and she suffered from depression. She knew it was her last speech as one of England's great-

Hilliard depicts Elizabeth in a dress representative of the late-Elizabethan style, which combines elements found in nature, such as flowers, animals, and fish.

est rulers. As she looked out at the members, Queen Elizabeth announced, "It is not my desire to live or reign longer than my life and reign shall be for your good. And though you have had, and may have, many mightier and wiser princes sitting in this seat, yet you never had, nor shall have, any that will love you better." Elizabeth I, always the Virgin Queen, died on March 24, 1603.

GLOSSARY

adultery Sexual intercourse between a married person and someone besides the husband or wife.

alliance Bond or connection between families, states, or individuals.

annulment Declaration that a marriage has ended legally.

behead To cut the head off of.

Commons A house of Parliament in England, similar to the US Congress.

concession Something granted.

dethrone To remove from a throne or place of power.

excommunicate Shut off officially from the rights of church membership.

heir A person who has a legal claim to a title or throne when the person holding it dies.

heresy A religious opinion that is opposed to Church beliefs.

illegitimate Born to a mother and a father who are not married.

imprison Put in prison.

mistress A woman who has sexual relations with a man who is not her husband.

moderate Opposed to major social change or extreme political ideas.

monarch A person who reigns over a kingdom or empire.

persecute Treat continually in a way meant to be cruel or harmful.

rebellion Open fighting against someone in charge.

reign Time when a king or queen rules.

treason Crime of trying to overthrow the government or hurting the ruler.

virgin A person who has not had sexual intercourse.

FOR FURTHER READING

Adams, Simon. *Elizabeth I: The Outcast Who Became England's Queen* (World History Biographies). Des Moines, IA: National Geographic Children's Books, 2008.

Eding, June. *Who Was Queen Elizabeth?* New York, NY: Grosset & Dunlap, 2008.

Ganeri, Anita and Rob Shone. *Elizabeth I: The Life of England's Renaissance Queen*. New York, NY: Rosen Publishing Group, Inc., 2005.

Harper, Meg. *Elizabeth I: The Story of the Last Tudor Queen*. London, UK: Bloomsbury Publishing, 2013.

Hollihan, Kerrie Logan. *Elizabeth I: The People's Queen*. Chicago, IL: Chicago Review Press, Inc., 2011.

Norton, Elizabeth. *The Anne Boleyn Papers*. Gloucestershire, UK: Amberley Publishing, 2013.

Pratt, Mary K. *Elizabeth I: English Renaissance Queen.* Edina, MN: ABDO, 2012.

Simmons, Michael W. *Elizabeth I: Legendary Queen of England*. Colorado Springs, CO: CreateSpace Independent Publishing Platform, 2016.

WEBSITES

Because of the changing nature of internet links, Rosen Publishing has developed an online list of websites related to the subject of this book. This site is updated regularly. Please use this link to access this list:

http://www.rosenlinks.com/WWCH/elizabethi

INDEX